THE KEY TO A SUCCESSFUL

BUSINESS

I really hope you like this book and it is able to guide you to a clear path into entering the world of business in the most effective way and from there gaining the right mind set to succeed.

If you do like the book, I will be most grateful if you could leave me a great review, no matter how small or big, which is the greatest satisfaction for me and encourages me to write more inspirational books!

ZAFAR ALI

Terms and Conditions

LEGAL NOTICE

Table of Contents

Foreword

They say that true success lies in doing business and not in pursuing better employment. And while it is true that some people who pursue better employment did achieve success, they are very few. After all, not everyone can be managers, supervisors, executives, and so forth and even then the higher up the ladder they go, the greater the responsibility, the targets and demands that are placed upon them lead to long working hours, immense work pressure and organizational competitiveness which can be debilitating. This in itself can have an immensely detrimental effect on their family lives and as we all know there is no end to the stories of stress, anxiety, depression, suicides, divorces, family breakdowns and so on.

Because of this, many people ditch the idea of employment and turn to entrepreneurship instead. And yes, it is true that many people did find success in doing business. And the sweetest part is that they get to be their own boss.

But just like in employment, not everyone who goes into business will succeed. In fact, there are probably more people who will fail than those who will succeed.

Yes, doing business is also a tough game. You must know 'the tricks of the trade' if you want to be successful. Does this mean that you have to get a college degree in business or marketing in order to be a successful entrepreneur? Well, that is definitely going to help. But there is a less time-consuming way.

Writing The *Key to a Successful Business* has been a determined effort. This book has been written with the intention of making people aware that being successful in business is not something that is too difficult to do, not with all the tools that we have at our disposal these days and are herein presented to you. They are not often shared, and the top entrepreneurs like to keep it that way, it's what gives them their competitive edge over the masses.

So what does having a successful business mean? Well for different people it means different things, but in this context we will take it to mean to having a business entity that provides us with enough money to meet our and our family's needs and not having to worry about where the next instalment or bill will be paid from, having a security of work and a steady income which allows extra capacity for us to be able to enjoy some of life's luxuries.

Most importantly, being successful is the power to be able to do what we want, when we want with the people who mean the most to us. This is what being successful really means. But, a lot of people have an entirely wrong idea.

They think it is an uphill struggle, out of their reach to become successful - they think they cannot do it without having some amazing skill set or some unique talent or getting a lucky break from somewhere, like winning the lottery or a substantial inheritance to help them along from a successful uncle or aunt.

But in reality lucky breaks seldom happen. Lucky breaks need to be created. Opportunities need to be created.

And this book is where you can learn how you can do that and how you can gain control of your own life.

In The *Key to a Successful Business*, the first thing you will learn is the corner stone of business, and that is having the right mindset, so in this book we start by fine tuning and improving that mindset, because that is the key to achieving positive outcomes in business.

Effectively you have to remove the thought of the inferiority complex that life around you has created and build on your confidence. You have to make adjustments in the way you think. Being successful does not require a supernatural talent in the way you might think.

It is all about putting the right effort in the right place. It is all about living your life, and planning your strategies, in the right manner at the right time, it is all about finding the right idea/opportunity that suits you and harnessing that opportunity in the most effective way.

Part I of this book takes you through that journey - a journey that tells you what you need to do in order to get there, but this book doesn't stop there.

Part II of this book goes on to show you the secret strategies to use once you are there, in a list not less than 70 key strategies used in almost any situation you will encounter once you get the ball rolling with your business.

The greatest and most significant invention in the business world right now and in fact potentially in the history of mankind is the Internet. Undeniably the Internet has seeped into every aspect of our being. We cannot refute that fact. And successful business people definitely do not forget that fact.

In fact, the successful business people of today are people who have harnessed the power of the Internet to make their lives better. They have grown, and they have expanded their businesses to never-before limits, with the help that the Internet world has provided them with.

For this reason Internet marketing forms a very important part of the discussions that you will find in this book. You will find that we talk about implementing the right marketing strategies and the right mind set or psychology that will elevate your position in this world and take you to the pedestal that many other people haven't reached before, at least not on such a sure footing.

One of the other things that have been given great importance too in this book is the art of reaching out to your niche.

Contrary to what most people think, the niche does not necessarily already exist. A Successful Businessman will create that niche.

They will develop the need for their product or service within a highly targeted group of people and that is how they tap into the vast potential that a highly targeted group of people or niche need or want.

In this book, you will see how you can create such a niche and/or even a niche within a niche within a niche.

In fact the narrower you go, generally speaking the higher your chances of success will be. Your demand will increase, and as the demand for your product increases, you will become a more successful business person.

Another very important thing is that you have to build a brand name not just for your business but also for yourself. You have to make yourself popular. You have to create a scenario in which even if you launch a new product or a new business, your name will pull it along and make it successful.

Like all other successful people out there, you should be able to run your business on the strength of your name alone. Taking you to the point that people should start trying to anticipate what your next product might be. Is that possible? Yes, this book tells you how you can achieve just that.

So, prepare to read this book. As you read it, keep your mind open. Let the ideas flow. The book will give you the raw material to have the right mindset, to think...but the eventual visualization and implementation must and will come from you.

And never forget the true world of business can be relentless. Let there be no doubt it is a place where success is rewarded and errors will be penalized. The benefit is that it keeps you realistic. You can't settle for helplessness, laziness, and bad ideas, or your business will collapse and you will fail.

That being said, you must never fear failure either, because the business wisdom you carry is partly a result of all your previous failures, each failure teaches you a valuable lesson and it is those lessons which brings you one step closer to your eventual success.

There's a huge chasm between a thought that sounds good and an idea that really gets carried out and succeeds under real life conditions. Anybody can muster up good ideas, but most individuals can't successfully follow through with them.

Some individuals can't handle the pressure of running their own business. They worry about the hazard of failure. They're viewing it from the improper angle though. That risk is exactly the point. Risk is what helps you grow. It makes you stronger and as stated above, failure should not be something you fear but something which is learnt from.

In fact failure is a crucial part of the journey towards the eventual success.

If you were to look at the global statistics of successful business people you will see a string of failures behind each and every one prior to the eventual success they eventually come to enjoy. And the one thing they all have in common is perseverance; regardless of the number of failures they continue to learn and move forward with the additional knowledge they have learnt from their previous failure.

Risk carries rewards, on the whole, the greater the risk, the greater the reward. However, that certainly does not mean that you should go all out and risk all that you have. As one would expect, risk is a serious thing, it should be carefully calculated. i.e. how much risk can you sensibly afford to take at any one time, considering not just the impact it would have on you but also on your family members too.

That being said a business person who dreads risk is like a muscleman who's afraid of barbells.

Unfortunately risk is part of parcel of achieving success in any venture.

The Key to a Successful Business

PART – I – Fundamentals of A Successful Business

Chapter 1: The 'Successful Business Person, Unsuccessful Business Person' Concept

Synopsis

Before starting out with this book, we need to know what the term The *Key to a Successful Business* means. It goes without saying, a business is an entity, the brains of the business is the person leading it and that is what will determine the direction and the eventual success or failure of any business.

This will help put everything in perspective.

In today's terms, a successful business person is someone who has access to different resources, and if he doesn't have immediate access he uses certain techniques to obtain those resources and utilize them effectively.

A good business person is someone who knows what it means to run a successful business and is able to cater for the market in the wisest manner.

A successful business person understands the importance of finances in business and at the same time does not over hesitate from making an investment when he sees a good opportunity, this could be either in improving the quality of an existing product or service or in the better promotion of a product or service to the market, because it is the enhancement of exiting products and services and their better promotion that will bring in more money which will ultimately allow him to do even more.

In essence, a successful business person is a person who knows what the market is all about and gives it what it wants. This helps the successful Business person to continue on the path of progress and move ahead in business pursuits.

So, where does the unsuccessful business person falter? The truth is that the unsuccessful business person has access to the same resources that the successful business person has, but the problem is that the unsuccessful business person either does not realise they are there or does not know how to effectively utilize them, thereby he has an existence in a world of tunnel vision.

The unsuccessful business person delves in ignorance, like the proverbial frog in the well.

The world has undergone a drastic change in the 21st Century.

Like in the feudal ages, the world is no longer divided into "haves" and "have nots".

The demarcation is not so simple anymore.

Today, in the world of information technology the true distinction is between the "knows" and the "know-nots", i.e. the people who know how to implement the methods that they have access to and the people who do not even know about these methods, or perhaps know about them but either forget about their implementation altogether or simply do not know how to implement them in the first place, and do nothing to understand how to implement them either.

This is what is truly creating the divide between the successful and the unsuccessful today and will continue to do so for years to come.

If you are reading between the lines, you will understand that the world of today has resources for everyone. Everything is there for the taking, for everyone to use. But, not everyone is using those things in the way they should or can.

This is what we are going to see in this chapter - the divide between the successful business person and the unsuccessful business person.

We are going to see what inspired us to come up with this concept. We will also see how the reality is true, in any age, but it is only the superficial aspects that tend to change from one era to another.

The 'Successful Business Person Unsuccessful Business Person' Concept - Where the Idea Stems From

With a plethora of information on "get successful quick" schemes and "self-help" aids, it is easy to get lost in the maze of who we should listen to and who to ignore.

Robert Kiyosaki of "Rich Dad Poor Dad" fame is certainly one person we could listen to; a founding member of the Elevation Group, he is one of those people who when they speak on a subject are worth listening too.

Why do I say that?

He has sat where so many of us are currently sitting, with so many questions about whether or not any business or investment decisions we make will actually make or lose us money, he has already trodden the path of indecision, risk and struggle.

He, like most of us, has sat facing unpaid bills and when the pressures of an income cannot sufficiently cover household and family expenses, he has learnt how to turn things around.

He has mastered the art of using the economic environment around us to make wealth and then use that wealth to make even more wealth.

The approach of this book is not a simple get successful quick scheme by any means, but it is a planned and focused approach to using the tools already in our hands to create a future that many can only dream about.

Education is the key to opening this door of opportunity. When I speak of education, I am not speaking about fancy university degrees or MBA's (even though I have one, and they do help too), but in this regard I am mainly speaking about the education of experience, of reflecting on the past, learning about trends and using them to gain valuable insights into the present and the future. As we do this in business and in our personal lives, we can turn around our financial affairs and reap the same rewards he has achieved in this process or at least some way towards it and maybe in other cases, more.

The aim of this book is to help ordinary people like you to achieve their dreams of a better future. The aim being not to stick with the status quo and not see gaining wealth as something negative but to seize the opportunity to find a better way of dealing with the resources and assets at your disposal.

This is a book for those who are thinking of either going into business or are already in business and who are seeking to use the various tools around them for their business success.

The book describes the importance of creating a niche-marketing environment. It explores the common problems people make in marketing and will assist you to identify your personal business niche. You will learn how to achieve an effective marketing strategy for your unique niche and how to use the proven principles to achieve dominance in a highly competitive market place.

Kiyosaki's Financial Precepts and Effective Marketing

Robert Kiyosaki, is a popular name all over the world. He is an American, a fourth-generation Japanese American, to be precise.

In the same style as his book, in this book I do not differentiate between the different ways in which one might carry on their moneymaking tactics. This book does not tell you to become a Business person or an investor or a marketer. Instead, the aim of this book is to tell you what you must do in order to attract more wealth doing whatever you are already doing. You will see that is what makes this book very special.

Kiyosaki has not spoken about marketing directly in any of his works, his perceptions are clear. He says that if you intend to have a great rapport with your clients, if you want to grow your business, then the one of the best ways in which you can do that is by increasing your network.

When your network is expanded, you can tap into it to make the most of your business. In the later chapters of this book I will show you exactly how you can do that.

This does require some effort though, and that is the reason why everyone is not into it. It takes special expertise as well. That is what separates the successful people from the not-so-successful ones. Proper networking is needed to reach out to a niche, which is where the real business prospects lie.

The Successful Business Person Unsuccessful Business Person Concept

My intention here is not to refute or criticize Kiyosaki's model, but to see how well it applies to the world of business as it stands today. Business is an entirely different ballgame - you may feel that it is so different from the individualistic approach that has been used in his books; but if you scratch the surface, then you begin to see the differences. In the main despite Kiyosaki's thinking, it is my opinion that marketing is critical for any business and therefore central to any business, as such the latter chapters of this book focus intensively on this area.

In this book, my focus is going to be on some key points.

1. We are going to see what it is that makes certain business people successful today. Yes, I must admit that I have a special fondness for Internet marketing, because this is the way the world is going right now. One of the best ways to become successful at present is by being successful in an Internet based environment, because that is what people can really use at a relatively low entry cost, at an individual or at

an organizational level, and to take them to higher realms of their potential.

2. Secondly, we are going to see that there are so many different things that successful business people do not wish to share with their unsuccessful counterparts, which in this case, are the people who have just started out and have still to carve a name for themselves in the business world.

It takes time; nothing is achieved without some effort, and there are many secrets that are being kept from the many. In short, what are the different things that are making the successful business people successful and are depriving the unsuccessful ones of the resources that these successful business people have access to?

3. The third aspect of this book is the possibility. Even if you are counted as an unsuccessful business person at present, there is no reason why you should not climb the ladder and go higher and become a successful business person yourself. You have the access to the same things that the successful business person has, except maybe you are lacking in the knowledge and information about them, so here is your resource to make the most of those things with the aim of levelling out the playing field.

4. That being said the most important thing that you would need is the better alignment of your mindset. You have to shun the thought of debilitation from your mind. There is no reason why you cannot go higher. Everyone started out somewhere first, everybody had a beginning, and in the business world, age is just a number. It does not matter what

age you are, you can go all out and popularize yourself immensely in the business world at any stage of your life, such is the power that is here and now, in the form of Social Media (which we will look at in more detail later).

Chapter 2: When Is a Niche Not a Niche in Marketing

Synopsis

One of the most important things that you need to know about being a successful business person is how to find a good niche and then how to tap into that niche. Your entire success depends on that. You need to know where your target customers are, what they need or want, how you will be able to focus on them and how you will be able to build on your prospects. This is the essence of business; there is no other truth beyond that.

That is the reason we have decided to clear the air about the concept of niche here. You need to know where your special forte is and you have to play to those strengths and interests. In fact, the better that you are able to do this, the greater the popularity you will achieve and bring the people to you that you need to promote your business to.

At the same time, you also need to be clear about the misconceptions of niche. There are business people who have an illusion of what their niche is. They think something is a niche when in fact it is an asset for someone else. Having a precise idea about your niche is what can help you to succeed in your business.

When Is a Niche Not a Niche in Marketing

"Survival of the Fittest" is not merely a topic for discussion in a science classroom. In a competitive business environment, only the business that is able to successfully market itself and its products and services to that niche will survive. Weaker ones will simply lose their customer base and eventually go into liquidation or bankruptcy. This is inevitable.

The Needs of the Niche

To gain a top marketing position and remain there, it is essential that the focus be narrow and the commitment be best determined. Without this approach, focus can become too broad and it becomes easy to spend time and money on too many things, none of which will provide the competitive edge the business needs to survive and grow. By creating a niche market focus, not only does a business define a place for itself and its products and services, but it is enabled to take advantage of an existing market for that niche.

Many businesses that promote a product or service believe they have a niche market, because of what they are seeking to sell or provide. While this is true to a certain degree, the focus may still be too broad for the marketing strategy to be considered a niche.

A true niche is not only the product or service being sold, it is also about the target audience of the advertising campaign. Advertising strategies are specifically pitched to customers who already are interested in the products and services on offer and actively searching to purchase or utilize them.

Most businesses market a large range of products to broad groups who may or may not be interested in what is being offered. Business strategies are often developed to advertise to a much broader potential customer base. By narrowing advertising strategies through a niche approach to marketing; valuable time, resources and money are not wasted. No matter how well advertising is presented, much of this style of advertising will only translate into a modest increase in customer numbers.

By focusing on the niche approach to marketing, the conversion rate of traffic to customers is much higher than for those businesses that focus on a broader marketplace.

The added benefit for those who enter into the niche market is smaller market competition to contend with and therefore a greater opportunity for faster success.

Finding your niche is the key to successful marketing and in the coming chapters, we will focus on how to identify your niche and how to market products and services to potentiate sales and profits. This approach to business also frees the business owner to be passionate about their product or service with people who are going to be interested in it.

The niche market is already an interested audience for your advertising campaigns. Niche marketing has the potential to give a business immediate marketing success.

The way one will create wealth is to understand that wealth comes from us and not to us. Wealth is a reward for services rendered. That is why you must help and truly give value to others and that's when you will attract people and greater wealth. If you focus only on money you will make just a living but if you focus on relationships, you'll make a fortune, that is the difference.

Niche marketing takes this principle and potentiates it in the business environment.

Identifying Your Niche

When you have realized the importance of a niche for your business, you will understand that there are various things that you need to do in order to identify it.

Your niche is the narrow area where your business has a competitive edge over other would be suppliers and therefore will focus on. It is the green pasture for you, the little area where you have the most lucrative prospects to take your business forward. This is the area where you know your business has a demand and is capable of providing a product or service better than others in some substantial way, and hence the prospects are high.

Instead of promoting your business to the whole wide world, just concentrating on this little niche market really makes sense, because here even if you market to only a 100 people, there is a chance that more than 80 people will view your business favorably, because you have already tapped into a market that is interested in you.

Conversely it makes sense that if you targeted your offering to a loose, wide majority without properly assessing your niche, then perhaps you would need to market to a 1000 people and maybe get say, 70 people interested.

Clearly that is a wastage of valuable resources, which would eat away at your profits and as such potentially render your business to run at a loss, even though in the above example the number of interested customers was very similar, you get the picture?

So it goes without saying, finding a niche, the right niche playing to your strengths is critical in business if you wish to be a successful business person.

Let us discuss some ways as to how you can find your niche:

1. One of the best ways to find your niche is to **follow your hobby or passion and convert it into a business**. This is a very easy thing to do and it will mostly come naturally to you because you are already more knowledgeable about your hobby than the mainstream and it would be fun to promote something that you are already excited about.

So, if your hobby is fishing, you could start a business about something relating to fishing, such as maybe making and selling fishing rods. Who is your niche in this case? Your niche is all the anglers of the world.

Doesn't it make perfect sense? When you are a hobbyist yourself, it is easier for you to get in touch with the other anglers of the world.

You know where they hang out, you know how to get in touch with them, and you know what will arouse their interest. In this case, you are a part of that niche, you are not apart from that niche, a critical distinction. It helps you to have a clear focus about what you are going to do and that can certainly help your business prospects.

2. You can also find a niche by **finding a specialized area of an existing market**. Take this example. The cell phone market is a huge market. Now, if you think of getting into the cell phone manufacturing market, that is a very huge task that you are planning to take up. Are you confident of meeting the demands of this very wide market? That is certainly a tall order! You only have to look at the players in that market to know the scale of who would be up against!

But here's the thing, suppose that you are able to narrow down your market. Instead of catering to the entire cell phone using fraternity, you decide that you will focus only on a part of it. You decide that you will specialize in making cell phones for the student market only.

In that case, you do not have to go too far. You only have to take a look at the needs, requirements and preferences of the student community and you create devices for them alone. You are not interested in the other users of cell phones and what they are looking for because that does not form a part of your niche market.

You only want to get in touch with people who are part of your niche.

Naturally, you will be able to produce more sophisticated products for this niche because you can do research on what this specific market needs and you will be better equipped to provide it to them.

3. Another way to identify a niche is to find out **a shortcoming or a lacking in an existing market**. When refrigerators were first invented, they were made of wooden or metallic bodies and they did not have the rubber

lining that they come with presently. Due to this, these refrigerators were immensely noisy and definitely not a pleasure to use.

Some smart cookie understood this shortcoming in refrigerators and then thought of a method to eliminate the noisy nuisance. Thus, the rubber lining was invented. You see the point... this was an add-on, something that was a failing of a previous product and now it has become a complete industry in itself.

Maybe you should take a look around as well. There are several products out there that need some kind of finesse. Also, there are several services out there that can do with some better planning. You do not need a scientific mind for that. Haven't you ever, after using a particular product or service, felt that if you had designed it, it would have been better?

4. Now is the time where you can use all these ideas and opinions and create a niche for yourself... likeminded people like you who are also looking for those very things that you purport to give to them and make some money in the process. **Something that is the need of the hour** could be an excellent niche for you to deal with. There are so many things that are lacking in the world that we live in. You should have a keen eye for finding out about those things. Then sit down and think...

why are those things lacking?

Can you do something about it?

Can you provide people with any solutions there?

In such cases, it might be required for you to up your skills somewhat. You might need to learn new things. You might need to invent something even. But do not let that faze you, that's part of the challenge, that's part of the journey.

The successful business people in the world, are those who have identified an unsatisfied need in the world and then fulfilled that need.

5. **Create a need.** This is perhaps the most difficult way of finding out your niche. It will take the greatest amount of creativity and effort. But, you can do it if you are given time. What did Bill Gates do? He created a niche, he created a need. He created a whole new niche of people who wanted to use computers. And that created a million sub-niches of its own.

You will need oodles of talent and inventiveness to develop a niche by creating a need. But, you should start by thinking about a new product... a product that will benefit mankind or nature in some way. You may have some ideas on that already. There are a lot more people with such ideas than you might think.

If you have something in your mind, do not nip it in the bud.

After you have carefully assessed the worth of that idea, think about what you can do to implement it. If you are sure, then you can go ahead and think about building on your concept and creating a need in the process.

Chapter 3: Building a Unique Niche Approach to Business

Synopsis

I f you really want to shine in your business, transition into becoming a successful business person, then you need to develop a unique niche approach to your business. Every business person needs to have a niche - we have already established that fact in the previous chapter - but to really stand out, you will need to have a niche that is unique. Your niche must be your own. That helps you build a stronger hold on the market because you do not have excessive competition. This kind of a monopoly position might be difficult to achieve, but once you have it, there is no stepping back. There is nothing that can deter you from going ahead from there on.

Building a Unique Niche Approach to Business

If you are already in business, you may already have a reasonable idea of what your unique niche already is. Most people enter into business, whatever its size, because they have an interest in the product or service they are selling. Perhaps you have qualifications within the industry your business operates or you have previously sold products and gained experience with the products you are now selling yourself.

Your niche is the primary product you are selling and the secondary products are those products that support the primary product. If you do not have a primary product, then your primary product should be the product you are currently ranking as your bestseller with customers.

If you are reading this book with the intention of starting your own business then consider the products or services that already have your personal interest. Investigate which of these are already in high demand with prospective customers. If you remain undecided about your business focus, choosing the product or service already in demand, will provide you with a potential niche focus.

Knowing which product or service to sell is at least in the early stages of developing a business, the easy stage.

The important point is not to grow your niche too big too quickly without having identified the niche group to market it too. Most businesses fail by trying to expand too quickly and without the customer base to support the expansion.

When determining how to market to your niche, it is tempting to try to take advantage of all the business and marketing tools one knows and develop strategies utilizing them. For instance, a classic mistake many marketers make is optimizing a website for search engines in the hope of attracting as many visitors as possible. This temptation may indeed attract more traffic to your website, but it is not necessarily going to mean those visitors will become customers who will remain loyal to your business or even have any real interest in your offering and this principle applies to all aspects of marketing.

When we remember, the role that developing relationships play in building wealth potential, it is easy to understand why statistics show that the best way to increase business is to develop relationships with your existing customers. This approach to customer service, contributes to customer loyalty to your products and services. Their word of mouth recommendation of your products and services will attract its own traffic.

Building a niche focus group does not mean not implementing optimization techniques to build a broader customer base, but rather encourages the resources and financial assets be directed towards an already interested market base. This enables the business to reward customer loyalty and build on existing relationships, rather than constantly needing to build new ones to maintain sales and profits.

The importance of this relationship approach to creating a customer niche is referred to as "wealth is a reward for services rendered".

In other words as businesses provide products and services to their customers, and customers recognize that, the business focus is one of providing them with what they want and need and are not just there for profit, they will return continuously and will bring other customers with them.

How Big Should Your Niche Be?

This is an important question that needs to be answered before you can plan anything concrete about your business. All your business related activities - strategies, business promotions, hiring people - will all depend on your niche. If your niche is very narrow, you will probably require only a few resources to bring it to fruition, but if your niche is huge, then you will probably need a large number of resources to make it happen.

That is the reason why you have to think about the size of your niche. Maybe you could begin by making a fair assessment of the kind of resources that you have at your disposal. What is the budget you have? How many people are working with you?

What is their expertise? What are your qualifications? What eligibilities do you have? And, most importantly, what are the visions that you have about your business?

These are the questions that you should ask yourself and get good answers to when you are planning on the size of your niche. You need to make sure that you select a size that works for you - a size in which you can fulfil your business's goals and ambitions.

Moreover, there is one very important thing. Whatever business you start with, one day you will need to expand it. At that time, you will want to widen your niche. That is why, even if you are choosing a small niche now, make sure that there is scope for growth. Your niche should be able to grow when you are ready for it. Will you be able to implement techniques that will help you find more people and/or capital to add to your niche, and hence aid you in growing your business?

The preliminary planning that you do for your business is what will dictate its future. At the same time do not to be too reserved/restrained in your thinking - there is a lot you can do if you visualize and plan well. So, let loose with an open mind!

Chapter 4: Marketing Strategies and Your Personal Niche

Synopsis

What you do with your chosen niche is a very important deciding factor for the way your business goes. Every business has a niche, whether they realize it consciously or not, and it is how they cater for that niche that matters the most. Now, every business has a different niche as well, that's the reason no two businesses can implement the same kind of marketing strategies. You will need to have an air of uniqueness about your marketing methods, just as your business niche itself is unique.

Here, pay close attention to this uniqueness factor, which is what can take businesses to the direction we want them to go.

In addition, in this chapter, we are going to discuss the popular marketing strategies that successful business people use today. These are the secrets that successful business people won't tell their unsuccessful counterparts, because they can do without the added competition. However, what they do not realize is that there is place for everyone. If you help others in the online world, they will help you too.

Why Do You Need a Unique Niche?

So, the mantra of any business is that it needs to have a well-defined niche that is its own. This is what helps it get an identity and establishes it in the industry.

Consider two credit card companies. Both have approximately the same features and are competitors. They are doing similar business as well. At present, both companies are working with the same niche. Then, one of the credit card companies introduces special cards for students.

This special student credit card has features like milder credit checks (which helps students because they do not have a credit rating yet), a lower spending limit (which helps students because they can manage their expenses better that way and ensure that they do not run long bills) and a low interest rate. Due to these features, this company wins over the trust of the student niche. Almost overnight, it overtakes its rival and its business improves.

This is an example in which a specialized niche can help your business. But let us take this example further.

Now, in order to still focus their attention on a closer niche, the company offers some added incentives to African-American students who want to take their credit cards. The niche becomes more concentrated now. These students go all out and order their credit cards, because they see this company's credit cards as solely made to cater for their needs and so do not even consider any other credit card. The business now spreads like wildfire in that niche, even if it is within a very small niche.

However, it still makes sense. By doing this the company has now actually monopolized credit cards in the African-American community. People from this niche are going to consider this company when they want credit cards and when they become professionals they will continue to stay loyal to this company.

To take it a step further, the credit card company introduces credit cards for the professional African-American community (as opposed to the student cards). As such the African-American community starts of becoming loyal whilst being students at University and then move on to the credit cards when they become professionals and furthermore they introduce other members of their community to this company's cards, both younger students and professionals of their community.

An intelligent move by this company is that it is catching people when they are young, when they are still students. Most of them are going to grow up and think about the great experience about the same company. So, even when they are more mature, the company has sold their credit cards to them from before.

In business, it is always the smarter cookie that turns out to be the successful business person. You have to be one step ahead of your competitors in order to win the rat race. Think what they are not offering to the market, then sit and plan your strategy to offer that very thing. Within the market, is there a group of people - on whom you can pay special attention and increase your business potential? Then why not do that. Go ahead with that group. This is your special niche. When you focus your attention on them, you are sure to multiply your business.

It is always wise to have 1,000 customers in a tight niche than have 1000 customers in a wide niche.

Can Your Business Niche Really Be Unique?

Now, the question is, can you have a unique niche? Is it possible to have that? Isn't it possible that your competitor has thought of it already?

These are the kinds of apprehensions that create hesitations in the minds of even the most prolific business people and hold them down. You cannot have such skepticism in your mind when you are trying to enter the successful business person category. Even if your competitor might have thought of this niche already, remember as yet, they have not tapped into it.

In the business world, it is always the first person who takes the step that counts, that builds the monopoly and ultimately gets to own that niche. This is the main reason why so many large corporations end up buying much smaller companies who own nothing more than a single niche in a huge global marketplace; rather than trying to enter that niche with a fresh offering of their own, these multinational corporations are well aware that the niche already has a well-established, successful small competitor in that niche, and that it would take too much time, effort and resources to try to capture that niche from that small competitor and it is far more efficient to simply buy out that niche owner.

When Alexander Graham Bell applied for the telephone patent, he was lucky because several other people applied for the same patent in the next few days. Their machines were almost the same as what Bell had devised, but still today we know Bell as the inventor of the telephone, not any of the others. Bell was also a great business person. He immediately got to selling his units and made a highly successful business out of it.

So, the timing surely matters. Something may be holding your competitors back, which is not your problem, because you haven't encountered it. There is no reason why a mere suspicion that your competitor may also be trying to enter into the niche should stop you from doing things.

To build your unique niche, these are the things you need to look for.

1. Think whether there is a special group within your larger group - a kind of subset within the universal set that you have been targeting for so long. What can you give to this special sub-niche? There might be some special features that they are looking for, they may have their own set of preferences and likes and dislikes. There might be some cultural points that you might consider as well. If there are things you can do that can help this special group feel more special, then why not go all out and give it to them? This could be your own, very unique niche.

2. Maybe you could look at your own personality, your own hobbies and passions. Consider an example. Maybe you are an artist; that is your hobby, not your profession. Your profession is that you are a fashion designer. Now, there are many fashion designers in the business and competition is certainly quite tough. But, you can plan something special. You are an artist, aren't you? You think of embellishing your T-shirts with your own artwork. You make unique artworks

and print them on the T-shirts and flood the market with them.

This can really get the people's attention. The strength lies in numbers too. When people can see these T-shirts prominently displayed, they are going to be interested in them. Just make sure not to go overboard though, because fashion should not be too commonplace. But, you get the point. Now you have something that your competitors don't have. You have an advantage and you are leveraging it on your business. In the meantime, your business is popularizing your artistic talent as well. You are aiming at two birds with one stone.

You have developed a special unique niche of your own - a niche of people who have become fans of your artwork. They wouldn't want anything else right now. You have a huge edge over your competitors. It just took you some thought to develop this subniche; you had the talent in you all the time.

3. There is another way to build a sub-niche. Are you associated with something that people know you for? Maybe you have done some charitable work for senior citizens in the past. Or maybe you are Jewish. Or something like that. If you have such a cultural, religious or linguistic edge, you have an opportunity there to create a sub-niche of people like you. Like attracts like in the world of business. Even today, in this highly liberal world that we are living in, people like to gather amidst other people who are similar to them. You might work this to your advantage in business. There is no harm in catering to a particular category of people; it is looked upon as philanthropy rather than sectarianism.

34

What Marketing Strategies Should You Adopt?

Once you have a unique niche, there is a very important thing that you have to think about. You have to think about how to reach out to this niche. Unless you are able to promote your activities to this special niche you have created, your efforts will be futile. Hence, a very important part of the job will be to implement proper marketing techniques to reach out to your niche, to popularize your business within the niche.

The following are some of the methods that you can use. In our subsequent chapters, we are going to see one of these methods - which we have handpicked to be the best in the current reckoning—in much greater detail. And, all of these methods are implementable on the Internet, because that is the weapon of the successful business person of today.

Popularize your product through articles. This strategy includes writing meaningful, informative articles and publishing them on the Internet across various directories. There are many article directories that will take your article submissions for free.

There are many advantages of writing articles on these directories.

1. First and foremost, you are giving out something to people for free - information. Most of the people in your market are looking for information right now. And, if you can give them this information for free, you are directly adding them to your fan base.

Also, by giving them relevant information, you are establishing your stamp of credibility on them. You are telling them, in no indefinite terms, that you know what you are talking about. You are showing them your expertise, and this makes you different, you are *the authority* on the subject.

You may notch up a good fan following of people who like to read your articles, and that is your unique niche right there. These people, who grow accustomed to your manner of giving information, will not want to buy products from anyone else.

2. The second marketing strategy, and this one is a personal favorite, is <u>blogging</u>. Have you tried blogging? This is perhaps the best way in which you can reach out to your unique niche and do the most of it. A blog is your personal space. It is the live recording of what you think and feel, in a chronicled manner. But, it is more than that. This is a place where people can read about you, and your business because that is our intention here, and they can post their comments. This has become a powerful tool of creating visibility over the Internet today.

In some ways blogs are the same as articles and in other ways different. Let me explain, they are the same in the manner that they contain relevant content. They are similarly text based and if you look just at the content on Notepad or something like that, you may not be able to tell whether the content will eventually land up on an article directory or a blog. But maybe the similarities end there. The reason is that blogs are highly interactive. When you are on a blog, it is possible for you to receive comments from your readers. They can read your blog posts, comment on them, and even share them with their own groups.

Blogs are the real new-age Internet marketing tools right now. They are so interactive that they can be shared through the Web via social media platforms and in many other ways. Each of these platforms is designed in such a way that they can popularize content on the Internet. Once you have a blog post on Facebook for example, the friends of the readers who like your content will be able to read it too. They will be able to like the content as well, which will add to its popularity. As a result, a lot of likeminded people are going to read your content and they may like the whole thing. With such social tools, you are growing your business at every minute or, to say it more precisely, you are growing your unique niche at every moment.

Surely this counts a lot for your business, doesn't it?

3. You may also want to try putting up press releases on the Internet. When you have devised a new product that you aim will cater to a new niche, or a special sub-niche within your existing niche, then you would do well if you put together or get a professional to put together a press release about it and submit it on a website like PR Web (http://www.prweb.com/), which is a press release directory.

Press releases are usually viewed favorably by the search engines because they contain updated information about something new that they feel people would like to know about. Hence, once you release a press release, people are immediately going to know about it. Services like Google's Google Alerts and Yahoo's Shine are instrumental in popularizing press releases to a greater extent, which means your chosen people are going to know very soon about what you want to tell them.

Internet press releases are different from offline press releases that you might find in newspapers and other publications. Internet press releases carry a direct link to your business webpages. Hence, people who are interested in what they read can directly come and visit your website. They can find out what your business is about, and carry on from there. Do not underestimate the power of a great press release in popularizing your business to your special niche.

4. <u>Email marketing</u> is another thing you have to consider. In this method, just as the name indicates, you send out emails to a group of targeted people. What are these emails about? You have to carefully design them so that they do not look spammy and they should contain enough meaningful content for your customers. They can contain some subtle marketing strategy within them, but on the face of it, they work the best if they look like they are part of a series or some tutorial that you are providing for free to your chosen target group.

You cannot send emails to people just like that. You will need to solicit their permission beforehand. Most of the successful marketers of the Internet today have done so by collaborating with popular websites and creating opt-in forms on these websites. When people become members on these websites, they are asked whether they would like information from their partners. People who agree to that are the people who opt in to get such emails. Once you have such a list of people, you can start sending them emails. You should not send too many emails - just 1 email per week or two should be sufficient to get your point across. Remember that you do not want to become a successful business person at the cost of sounding too desperate. Also, build a powerful strategy right at the start. Once you have your strategy, do not shift from your path.

You might have 10, 20 or 40 emails in a series - it does not matter, but it is necessary that there is a common strand connecting them all.

You can make the most out of your email series by using autoresponders. Autoresponders are automated messages that are sent out to someone when they take a particular action. For example, people may get an automated message as soon as they opt in to your service. This message invites them to the group. You can have more automated messages later on during the course. In fact, you can schedule the entire email series to be sent out through autoresponders.

Your competitors are doing it already, and if you want to become a successful business person, you need to use these techniques before they do. Also, email marketing is a wonderful way to personally contact people from your unique group, which makes them feel special and they start thinking quite favorably about you.

5. Another important marketing strategy that you need to consider in order to connect with your unique niche is to build a great <u>sales page</u> setting out what you do. This sales page could be as long or as short as you want, and you can make it as creative as you want too. A sales page is a blatantly promotional page, so it is very different from all the other methods I have discussed with you, but it can hit the mark if well thought out and you plan it well.

Basically, your sales page should tell people what your business is about. You need not tell them all the details right away, but your sales page could be a way of giving them a good preliminary idea about your business. You could consolidate your sales page by giving people an option to opt in to some list so that they can be kept in the loop for further information.

Remember people do not always buy the first time they see something, often they need to think about it, discuss and mull over it, but unfortunately people also have very short memories and soon forget all about your product and move on to other things. The emails act as a constant reminder and a connection with those that once showed interest.

The above example also highlights an important point in that, the various marketing techniques are not entirely independent of each other, but a mix of tools should be used and there should be interconnections between them.

Today, marketers are designing immensely different sales pages, using all the creativity they can. It is possible to have audio clips and video clips in a sales page. There are also people images that can crop up from the bottom right of the screen announcing the product and speaking to people about it that can be placed on the sales page.

There are links to other social networking places (see below) that you can put on the sales page, where people can go visit and find out more about you.

But, what really puts the icing on the cake on the sales pages are testimonials. It is important to try to get good testimonials from your existing clients and put them on your sales page. This really makes the difference. People understand that your product is something worth considering because there are a lot of happy people who have used the product. Even here, you have ways to be unique. You could add video testimonials from people, this is the holy grail of the thumbs up for your products!

6. Keeping on the theme of videos, do not underestimate the power of videos as a very interesting and highly effective way to make your business reach out to your chosen niche, referred to as <u>video marketing</u>. You can try this method out. Make a short video about yourself saying something about your business - it could be some kind of a tutorial video, or it could be a review, or it could just be an interview - anything you like. Once you have such a video, put it up on websites such as YouTube or Daily Motion.

You will almost immediately see the jump in sales. Right now, YouTube is second only to Google as the most popular search engine. People are coming here to find information. In fact, they are coming here to look for videos.

When you make meaningful videos and post them on YouTube, you can get very popular. Your credibility is increasing.

Furthermore, you can add links to your business within these videos. People can visit your website once they have liked your video; it is as simple as that.

You can see the immense advantages of having a video about yourself or your business. You are automatically increasing your popularity by leaps and bounds. You are becoming some kind of Internet celebrity and you are stamping your credentials. People will trust you as a reliable source for information and as an authority, provided you post good content. And, since you are trying to locate your special niche within the niche, this is the method that can take you there.

7. You can try out <u>affiliate marketing</u>. This is one of the ways in which you can go out and reach your unique niche. When you are marketing through your affiliates, essentially you are placing an ad of your business on their websites, blogs or whatever. These people are generally those who have businesses related to yours. Thus, they have a good chance of bringing in your special niche to you.

For example, if you have a business of selling pregnancy wear, then a website that gives pregnancy self-help information could be your affiliate website. You could put up an ad of your business on their website. When women come looking on that website for information about their pregnancy, they will see your ad and potentially click on it to visit your website as well. That is how simple it is to bring an interested person over to your website through affiliate marketing.

Affiliate means to associate with or be a member of something or someone. This means that affiliate marketing can be considered as a business that gives compensation or a reward for a person who brings another client into the business. There are many examples of affiliate marketing available both online and offline. One example is whereby a client is giving a certain money back coupon when they refer another client to the vendor of a good or service.

Other examples are when a person is given gifts in form of cash or other rewards for referring people to the vendor. These examples are the reason why some people earn some money using affiliate marketing. Affiliate marketing is done through using certain levels.

The levels are mainly four which can be used to make affiliate marketing a success. In the first level there is the merchant or vendor. From the vendor, the next levels are the network, the publisher and the affiliate.

These steps of marketing have an indirect connection with internet marketing at some point. This is attributed to the use of regular advertising methods by affiliates to get other affiliates.

Advertising methods that affiliates use will include email marketing, display advertising, search engine marketing and search engine optimization. One form of strategic affiliate marketing is by using one website to drive and send traffic to another. This is one of the methods of Internet marketing that is normally unseen by advertisers.

Other modes of online marketing are predominant than affiliate marketing. It is still on a low profile despite the fact that it is a big part of online marketing.

There are some compensation methods that are normally made using affiliate marketing. These compensation methods given to affiliates are different and understanding them would be advisable.

The methods are:-

- Predominant Compensation Methods

- Diminished Compensation

- Performance Marketing

- Multitier Programs

Predominant Compensation Methods

When these types of compensation methods are used, there is the revenue sharing and cost per share that is given. The percentage of programs that use Cost per Share (CPS) is 80%. 19% of the programs compensate on a Cost per Action (CPA) method. The remaining percentage is normally used by Cost per Mille (CPM) and Cost per Click (CPC).

Diminished Compensation Methods

Markets that are mature use a different mode of compensation. Less than 1% of these traditional affiliate programs currently use CPC and CPM. Such kinds of compensation procedures are mainly used in paid searches and display advertising. CPM will require the party advertising to avail the advert on the site and display it to visitors so that they can get a commission. When PPC (Pay per Click) is used, there is another step that has to be accomplished in order to receive compensation. It will require the visitor not only to view the advertisement, but also to click on it.

On clicking the advertisement, they are directed to the advertiser's website. CPC had a lot of popularity when affiliate marketing was starting.

However, there has been a continuous rise in click fraud such that the method is seen as an easy way to defraud some money from the Internet. Though some of these methods have had a decrease in popularity in some areas, there are some which are still being used in other areas. A good example of an area that still uses these methods is China. When compared to the West, it has a different system to compensate affiliates. Most of the affiliates are being paid on a Cost per Day basis. Some of the networks in China will offer CPC and CPM despite the reasons stated above.

Performance Marketing

In CPM and CPC, the publisher will not be interested by a visitor becoming a member of the audience that an advertiser is trying to target. The reason behind this is that the publisher will already have gotten their commission. As a result, a lot of loss and risk is left to the advertiser if a visitor cannot be converted. In most cases, the highest risk is seen in CPM.

CPS and CPA require the referred visitors to do more than just look at the website that thy have been referred to in order to receive a commission. The advertiser has to make sure that the visitor is converted. To make a conversion, an affiliate will have to send traffic that is targeted to the advertiser. This way, they have a higher chance of making a conversion. Risk and loss in this situation is shared between the advertiser and the affiliate.

In some cases, affiliate marketing can be termed as performance marketing. The term is used in reference to the compensation of the employees. Most of these employees are paid by commission. However, there are added bonuses for performing more than the baseline which they were given.

Affiliate marketing has been compared to be a sales team. This is not true for two reasons. The first reason is that a person who is an affiliate marketer provides very little influence on a possible prospect. Secondly, an advertiser will not have any control over any prospect.

Multitier Programs

These type of programs give commissions on a hierarchical referral network. Such programs are normally referred to as multitier programs. A good example of the same is when a publisher, say publisher "1", gets a contact with an advertiser. Once publisher 1 gets this contract, he/she will get other publishers which we will call "2" and "3" to sign up through him/her. The two new publishers will sign up for the same system or program using the code that publisher "1" gave them.

Once they have signed up, any earnings that publishers "2" and "3" get in future will be paid to them but an additional commission (though at a lower rate) will also be paid to publisher "1".

Very few affiliate programs have a two tier program. Those that are more than one tier are more or less like Multi-Level Marketing (MLM) programs. However, MLM seems to have a higher qualification and complex commission systems than normal affiliate programs do.

There is a payment necessary though. You will have to pay your affiliates for promoting you. Generally, you pay them according to the number of clicks that these people are able to divert to your business. You could use a reliable service like Google AdSense. This service automates the entire process on your behalf and you can easily find out how many clicks a particular affiliate has sent you and you simply pay Google AdSense in accordance to that.

But the big benefit of affiliate marketing is that you are bringing people over to your website, and these are people who are connected to the niche that you are planning to target.

8. However, if you really want to walk over the competition, then the method that you should seriously consider is <u>social networking</u>. This is age of social networking. Everyone is one these websites right now, connecting with each other like never before. There are groups of people here, people sharing likes and dislikes and having common interests and preferences. People making recommendations to others, you want to be amongst those recommendations.

If you could attract one of these people within a social networking group, then you have a chance to attract so many more. Their entire friend's group could be yours for the taking. When you are have a good product or service and good reviews from people who have used it, viral marketing through such social networking websites is something that could make you into a very successful business person. People will like your stuff and then recommend it to others. This kind of popularity can increase with amazing alacrity. You will be surprised at the prospects you build up even when you are sleeping.

Social networking is so huge, such a powerful tool, that you just cannot ignore it if you want to become a successful business person. In the next chapters, we are going to take a closer look at social networking and how it can make you a successful business person. We are also going to look in detail at three of the major social networking websites.

Chapter 5: Social Networking and Niche Marketing

Synopsis

Quite assuredly, this is the age of social networking. People are using the Internet as a tool to get in touch with others. Even people living within the same house add each other to their social networking groups. The reason is that there are so many assorted activities that you can do here that it becomes a fun-filled rollercoaster ride rather than just being a means of communication. People are on each other's social networks much more than ever before, and the successful business person is definitely on board with that.

Over the last few years, successful business people have gone out and created a very strong presence in the social networking world. They have built niches within niches, and they have multiplied their marketing practices many times by creating a strong interactive base on these social networking websites.

If you want to make the transition to being the successful business person as well, you need to understand this fact well. You need to jump up and reach the higher grapes if you want to be special, and in this case, that means the added effort that you might have to put in so that you can make a presence on the social networking websites. At the end of the day, you will find that this really helps you to find connect with your niche, and not only that, you will be able to impress them with what you can do.

You can make people within a social networking group your fan base. You can make these people look up to you for information and reliable resources to do things they want to do. If you are able to work on the trust factor in this manner, you will be able to actually reach out and convert them to becoming your customers, which is one of the most important things for you to do if you want to become a successful business person.

Social Networking and Niche Marketing

Creating niche traffic by advertising on social network sites such as Facebook, Twitter, YouTube and LinkedIn is a convenient and easy way to create a network of people who are interested in your services and products.

Advertising campaigns promoted through social networks target products and services to a customer base that is more likely to be receptive to them. Customers choose to join your network because they believe they will benefit from the contact with you and your services or products. You are now in a position to capitalize on that trust relationship and provide them with those "extra mile" services that will reward them for their loyalty to your business.

Providing those on your networks with ongoing information and resources will maintain their trust that you are a market leader and therefore a trusted provider of quality goods and services. This more personal contact with the business representatives and the business itself, helps to keep the business relevant to its customers.

Evidence for the success of social networking sites as an important business strategy, is its use by celebrities, companies and other corporations to stimulate interest in their activities and products. Television channels for example, use social media sites to create interest in their regular television programs and this helps them to maintain top ratings for some shows and to improve ratings for others. Politicians are increasingly using social networking as tools for their campaigns, highlighting their ability to communicate to a broad spectrum of supporters in a cost effective and efficient manner.

The advantage of social networking is the ability of informal and formal dialogue to take place between business and target audience in real time and supported by use of video and photo technology.

A strong social network also enables business to link with likeminded businesses and share resources and knowledge of current market trends. In the past, this knowledge has helped market leaders make predictions that have guided and driven their business decisions. Creating these networking relationships has the added benefit of providing back links to your website from other websites, an important strategy for Search Engine Optimization.

There is clear evidence of the success of social networking as an important marketing strategy for a niche business, When it fails it is often because there have been no strategies developed to maximize the benefits of using this medium. The goal is to actively engage people with you and your products and services so they are regularly updated with not only descriptions, but also with practical ways of using them. This information when tagged with back links to your website will potentially draw a loyal customer base to your website regularly. This traffic will create more sales, than conventional advertising. A sensible approach is to dedicate someone (a team if possible) to completely focus on the social networking activities and monitoring of such.

Because the content on our social networking site is focused on a niche market, it must focus only on the products and services you are providing and should not include other content, which is not directly related in some way to your business focus.

Social networking is possibly the key strategic action you can take to create an environment to sell your products and services. With careful planning, social networking offers you a more consistent approach to advertising and building a niche customer base, than most other forms of advertising and network building.

The Big Social Networks

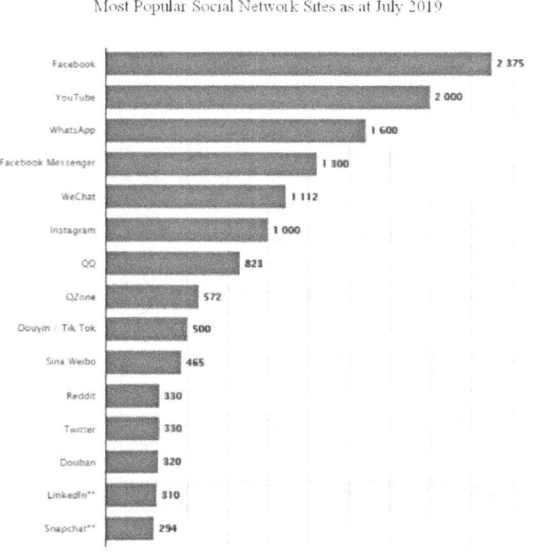

Most Popular Social Network Sites as at July 2019

The statistic provides information on the most popular networks worldwide as of July 2019, ranked by number of active accounts. Market leader Facebook was the first social network to surpass 1 billion registered accounts and currently sits at almost 2.38 billion monthly users. Sixth ranked photo sharing site Instagram had 1 billion monthly active accounts.

There are countless social networking sites, but a few as shown in the infographic above have overshadowed all the others. There are three social networks which are particularly good for businesses and also for building relationships, these being Twitter, Facebook and LinkedIn.

Together social networks have given the concept of global village a new dimension; people from all over the world are tied together in one place sharing their life's experiences, ideologies, cultures and even business now. These social networking sites have introduced a new pattern of business by converting a serious medium of business into a social, lighter, and fun filled medium but its objectives are still the same. They are also playing an important role as an online recruitment network.

These days, one of the most prominent social networking sites is Facebook. Currently, it is the most viewed and used social networking site almost 3 billion visitors every month. Initially it was made for young students to share their updates, pictures, videos and other content with their friends and family members but within a few years it has become the biggest craze in the world. People have become addicted to Facebook. Many new friendships and relationships have been formed through Facebook. It is not only limited to social networking with friends and family but it also allows people to make their company pages and other social groups to exchange information about their business.

Promotion of companies and organizations and advertisements at affordable prices on Facebook is huge. It has opened up many opportunities for various new jobs as well, and has become the most popular and successful social network of the day, as such it cannot be ignored.

Twitter is no doubt the most powerful micro blogging network to date where people connect with the followers of the same interests instantly. It has an excellent quality where people can send instant messages to other people of their interest. It provides a better opportunity to socialize. Trend or popularity is increasing day by day with approximately 330 million visitors every month.

Twitter is popular with famous celebrities and personalities, journalists and of late even very famous politicians who like to tweet about their upcoming projects, personal and controversial matters. Unlike Facebook, it is not necessary to add people in your friends list to socialize with them; it allows you to message, well, anyone without following them. Here, you can meet new people every day, interact with the people of your niche and can share or market your business as well.

Contrary to the above two social networks, LinkedIn is the smallest but more of a professional site with better recruitment opportunities. Here, a person builds their profile, uploads their CV and qualifications, and then adds their friends and other professional companies related to their interest or field as connections. Here, people can find more opportunities to contact with more senior and experienced professionals. Most companies hire through this social network. Its popularity is increasing rapidly. According to the estimation, its monthly traffic is around 310 million.

Therefore, apart from all the other social networking sites these are three of the big social networks in 2020, working tremendously with increasing revenue per day and providing more opportunities for business and social networking around the globe.

In the further chapters, we are going to take a closer look at each of these three top 3 social networking websites that have revolutionized the world of niche marketing.

Chapter 6: Facebook Marketing - Mingling Business with Social Activities

Synopsis

Facebook is the most popular social networking website today. Strictly speaking, Facebook is not designed for business, but that does not deter the successful business person from using it for business. The very fact that Facebook has such a lot of people on it at any given moment of the day and the fact that there are a large number of apps that it is associated with makes it an option that successful business people just cannot ignore.

Successful business people are using Facebook to create their social networking presence, and even domination. They are building their own little groups where they are popularizing themselves and then they are creating their monopoly.

This is happening to such an extent that they are becoming go-to resources for people from all over the world who are trying to look for specific information.

You cannot ignore such a huge phenomenon that has swept the world in such an emphatic manner. This chapter tells you what this phenomenon is all about, and how marketers can use it to leverage their presence in the online world.

Facebook Marketing Mingling Business with Social Activities

Facebook is the most popular social networking site with a monthly traffic of almost 3 billion. It is the best possible way for marketing today. Facebook was started as a social networking site for college going students to interact socially with each other and share their activities, photos and videos.

Facebook is not only limited to social networking; it has now become the most powerful marketing site as well. It has started mingling business with other social activities very smartly and strategically.

Facebook is used for the marketing of various products and companies. Different pages and profiles have been made to promote different companies and personalities.

In order to promote through different pages on Facebook, people make a specific page of their company and put their necessary information there. They use different tactics to make their page more attractive and popular like using an attractive profile picture, continuous updates about the products of the company and by adding new friends and requesting them to like their page. Through this kind of marketing, a person or representation of the company, like a PR man, establishes his own identity, along with the company's information in front of the people. They keep on connecting with more and more people so that the social network increases rapidly, it is a bit like domino effect.

As people visit or like a page, the publicity of the product increases. Online description and display of new products creates awareness. Apart from that, the option of invitation to official or social events has played a significant role in mingling business with social activities. People make invitees of their events through Facebook and save their money as it is free of cost here. Put simply Facebook is the most economical, easiest, fastest and successful mode of promoting business.

Facebook is all about getting new advertisements on affordable rates on a daily basis; the promotion of additional company websites, company divisions and company individuals can be done through Facebook.

It is also used for the promotion of other website's content by integrating Facebook plugins on different websites like sharing of clips from YouTube through these plugins. Apart from that, other online articles and videos from various websites are also posted on Facebook. This has increased Facebook marketing.

Facebook has given a whole new meaning to the business promotion and marketing by converting a serious business medium into a social and interactive medium. Common people find it easier to promote their new business through Facebook than any other medium. Facebook has its own 'Marketplace' page where masses can sell and purchase different things. This application page shows all the recent listings in your profile. This is more attractive than other pages and provides you with a complete range of products related to you and people in your network directly or indirectly.

In essence, Facebook is a medium which allows the mixing of business with social networking through joining or liking the business page of friends and friends of friends as well. Through this, more and more people get associated with your business directly and indirectly. It is for that reason that Facebook is considered a very successful medium of marketing.

Chapter 7: Twitter Marketing - Tweeting for Business

Synopsis

Twitter is another very popular social networking resource that works on a totally different concept. This resource has become popular due to its use of micro-blogging. You can post small bits of content here, generally known as micro-blogs and tweets in particular, that tell people what you are doing or what you want to tell everybody. You can give people links to your business. You can create a base of people who follow you. Your followers can be followed by other followers. In a very short time, you could have a large number of people who are following what you say on Twitter.

That can work amazingly well. These people have decided to follow you. So, by implication, these people are interested in what you want to say. They have faith in your tweets.

Hence, the successful business people will never want to lose out on this opportunity. Tweeting for business is what everyone is doing right now, and this is one area you should focus on as well.

Twitter Marketing - Tweeting for Business

Business in today's world is no longer just limited to offices, documentations and business meetings. It is more global and social now; tweeting for business is an interesting concept. Twitter provides a platform to the people in business to make more contacts and do marketing of their company and products.

Twitter is a micro blogging site where people can do promotions but shameless and obsolete marketing is not allowed. It is not a way of starting or promoting a business. It is only a platform to promote your own self, your ideas and new products. It is used for forwarding your business rather than launching it.

All you need to do is register and log on to Twitter and then start following someone, giving you the capability to show your likes and dislikes. Furthermore you are free to tweet others, give feedback and opinions on different subjects as long as it is within the 280 character limit.

Due to the sheer nature of the site and hence the character limitation, your tweet should be crisp, short and unique. By posting your comments and feedbacks, you are showing your presence there. It is necessary that you develop a social interaction with different people on the site. If you do not interact with them and only post your ads then people might think that you are nothing more than a hard salesman. Make healthy relations with people so that they start following you. Only then will you be successful in convincing people about your business and products.

Tweeting for business is like establishing a brand image. For example, when a specific brand is being launched the manufacturer uses many different ways to promote it and make people well aware about the brand. Advertisements also use the same technique, like they don't sell brands but they sell ideas. People usually accept and adopt them as a part of their life styles. Only after building an emotional relationship with the product, the brand loyalty develops among the consumer. Similarly for promotion of business, you must build a relationship of trust with your followers and Twitter is the best available platform for this purpose. Writing a profile with your biography is the first and most important step, so that people know about your qualifications, experiences and business and people will start following you.

Following which, you should keep on tweeting on other tweets. Do not hesitate to express your opinions and point of views on different subjects. If you do not agree with something, feel free to disagree but don't be rude; selection of words should be careful. Build arguments and support your point of view with solid proofs and statements. It will show others that you have some knowledge and you have an ability to be determined to your beliefs. This will definitely increase your followership.

Keep contact with your followers, discuss things with them, share your ideas about promotion of your business and fields of your interest, point out what your business does, don't fear to give statements and don't be afraid of opposition. Put questions to others; it is a platform for two way communication and their responses will appear as a review for clients and followers. Always share links and informative things on Twitter and ask people to follow, this is good practice and the journey to success on this platform.

Hence, tweeting for business is an excellent way to compliment your company and show the Internet presence. Note the key differences between Twitter and other social networks, in the main do not confuse it with the other social networking sites or just any other business site.

Chapter 8: LinkedIn Marketing - Building a Strong Online Reputation

Synopsis

L inkedIn is the place to build a professional profile. You can write about yourself, build a resume for yourself, a profile for your business and go on to build your great online presence. When you have a substantial profile for your business, you will be able to reach out to the right people, and the right people will get interested in you as well.

LinkedIn is a very successful resource to build contacts. We shall see how this social network can be utilized to get in touch with other likeminded people and let them know of your expertise. If you want to monopolize, a good LinkedIn profile that speaks for itself can go some way towards that.

Building a Strong Online Reputation Through LinkedIn

LinkedIn is a powerful way used in the Internet today for establishing professional relationships. If Facebook and Twitter are famous for being powerful social networking sites, then LinkedIn is considered the best for professional networking. It has almost 310 million users per month.

You can use your LinkedIn profile as a very powerful tool to establish yourself on the Internet. It is very helpful in building a strong reputation online professionally. After registering into LinkedIn, create your profile. You upload your resume after that.

The most important step to make LinkedIn profile as your online resume is to state your summary strongly. The summary must be written in your own words. Mention why you think that you are the best in your specified profession and why others should consider working with you. It is more like a covering letter for yourself in front of the world to convince them to take on your expert services. The summary should be compact and effective. Use strong key words to describe your professional qualifications so that it will become easy for other likeminded professionals to find you.

Use LinkedIn as a profile to explain about your past experiences in detail. Write about your qualifications in a well written or specified form so that it attracts the readers. Never exaggerate your good points. It should not seem that you are self-obsessed. Write an accomplished matter that will set you apart from others. Try to get recommendations from those professional or experienced workers with whom you have even worked before or have some links. Recommendations will increase your chances of getting better opportunities.

Do come up with your customized vanity URL, as it is quite helpful in building your reputation online because whenever people want to search you, they will use Google easily. Join all the relevant groups in LinkedIn which are related to your qualifications and interests; it will help in building your resume with a better outlook and impact.

If you are on LinkedIn, then you have fair chances of starting your own blog as well. In LinkedIn, there is a web section that allows you to share your web accounts very easily.

Apart from the web sections and blogs, LinkedIn provides access to Twitter which allows the sharing of tweets on LinkedIn. It is not like the other social networking sites where you may write about feelings and such. LinkedIn is more professional and business orientated.

Therefore, LinkedIn helps in building a strong reputation online which further helps you in getting more professional assistance and opportunities to prove your potentials. The employers who recommend you can be requested to write testimonials for you. This way, it will help you in building a strong and professional reputation on LinkedIn, which further aids in making your online resume stronger and more attractive to new recruiters.

Chapter 9: Building a Powerful Business Presence Regardless of Any Economic Environment

Synopsis

It is no secret - all is not so well with the world in the current scenario. It hasn't been so for the last few years. This is putting a spanner in the works. It is keeping enterprising people from reaching where they want to reach. If you want to become a successful business person, the economic climate may not be conducive to you at this time.

But that is what being a successful business person is all about. They have various secrets up their sleeve. They know what they can do to turn the tide in their favour in any climate.

In this optimistic chapter, we are going to see how we can do just that; turn the tide in our favor despite the complications that the present global financial situation may put in our path.

Building a Powerful Presence Regardless of Any Economic Situation

Many people are reconsidering their dreams of having a successful business of their own. They look around, see evidence of bankruptcies, and wonder about the wisdom of moving from secure employment into the unknown of self-employment.

Statistics would certainly suggest that this is a good idea; most small businesses shut down after a few years or are sold for much less than the business is worth. This however, does not need to be the case. A business can be described as the establishment of the business a journey or a process. It will have a beginning, an end, and a lot of work in the middle.

A good business is the one that creates income, without endless effort on the part of the business owner. The business itself creates the wealth. It may take time to establish, but once established it continuously makes money for the owner.

The process is the key to building a powerful business presence despite any current economic climate. Now while it is true that dreams do not make the business succeed it is equally true that without dreams business won't succeed. Once you own your dream, you can then build your plans.

Planning is essential because without planning there can be no progress. Plans provide the blue print for the business operation.

However although most businesses have a business plan the reality is they do fail. Planning by itself is not enough to prevent failure. The difference between a successful business and one that fails is the reaction of the business owner when the inevitable problems occur and what the owner does when facing failure.

It is inevitable that mistakes will be made. Many people hit a shaky place in their business dealings, and scared off by the situation will at this point choose to close their businesses.

However it is important that one is not deterred by such downs and keep going and creating learning opportunities from these mistakes. Instead of despairing, let the mistakes drive you to learn why any failings are happening and think about what you could and can do differently to prevent that from happening again. Seek answers in many places.

Making the commitment not to give up is only the first stage in becoming a powerful business presence. Building networks and focusing on services rather than just producing an income source are essential.

Nevertheless, it is important to understand the various forms of income, and there are three ways money can be earned:

1. Personal Income

2. Portfolio Income

3. Passive Income

Most people focus on personal income, however, I encourage readers to focus instead on the other sources of income, personal income is dependent on time and effort from the person earning it, whereas the other forms of income require little effort and money is being made, even when the person is sleeping and this is the crux of the matter, as the truly successful business people create businesses which earn money for them around the clock and around the year.

How does the principle apply to businesses? Most people put their effort and money into making the business earn the money, whereas the focus should be on creating the niche and creating the network to promote your offering within that niche. This will make more money than focusing resources and effort on the business itself.

Do not create business plans that require you to work hard to create money, but focus your attention on creating business plans where investing and passive income sources do the work for you.

Chapter 10: Ten Things Successful Marketers Hide from Their Unsuccessful Counterparts

Synopsis

In this chapter of *The Key to a Successful Business* book, we see some of the things that the successful business people try to keep away from the unsuccessful business people. As you read these things, you will find out that there is not much that people do not know, it is only that the successful business people utilize these things earlier and try to dominate them. If you want to make the transition from being an unsuccessful business person to being a successful business person, then you should read the following points quite closely.

Ten Things Successful Marketers Hide from Their Unsuccessful Counterparts

Many of those who today are well-known business people, successful and mega successful have one thing in common with each other. Each of them was at one stage either an unsuccessful, struggling student or a bankrupt business person from some previous business, just think of Larry Page and Sergey Brin (creators and owners of Google), or Alan Sugar, the reputable UK billionaire, who started life in a council flat selling car aerials and other consumer electronics from the back of a van.

But from there they started with a dream, an idea that began as a spark and that spark of an idea grew into the multimillion-dollar companies with which their names are synonymous.

What created the success for them? What was the key to their success when so many others have failed?

i. They had a dream and they lived that dream and did not give up on that dream. That dream was a big dream and it drove them. They believed their dream even when failure stared at them in the face.

ii. They learned from their mistakes and turned mistakes into wisdom and that wisdom into success. They used failure as a learning tool to enable them to consider how to do things better the next time.

iii. They started small and gradually built up. Their focus was on building a niche and being the best in that niche. They did not allow their focus to become too big too quickly. This is the sure recipe for success.

iv. Their focus was not on the income but on the product and building a loyal base of supporters through the product (or service) they were offering. Networking was the key, it produced the market, and it produced the opportunity for expansion. They did not need to do it alone. Others bought into their dream.

v. They explored and utilized every available marketing strategy to build their dreams, with the focus firmly on building social networks to develop strong customer focused and customer driven products and services, such that the products sold themselves.

vi.   They invested time and energy into the development of businesses that eventually produced income with little or no effort on their part.

vii.   They explored and understood social and economic trends to ensure they understood where the market was going and historically what to expect, understanding that history often repeats itself.

viii.   They focused their time, energy, and resources on the outcomes of their research, and invested accordingly, rather than following the crowd.

ix.   Although at times they did hesitate, they kept the dream alive and did not allow setbacks to destroy that dream, but having learned from the setback, they allowed themselves to continue the dream and take risks.

x.   As they took risks, they did not lose sight of their objective to create successful businesses and have an income source that did not rely totally on their involvement to be successful and they continued to do that once they became successful – this principle is visually highlighted in the BBC TV program 'Dragon's Den'.

Those who have failed in business are those who have allowed the business environment to force them to make decisions whilst they have failed to do their own research.

They do not understand the rise and fall of the markets and the wealth cycles. This has prevented them taking full advantage of investments and portfolios that create income and even lose what income they have earned. They have accumulated debt rather than focusing on escaping the debt cycle and failed to see the money market for what it is.

They have succumbed to their failures and been scared off by them and they have given into the market trend that suggests that you cannot make money as a business person.

Part I - Wrapping Up

In writing The Key to a Successful Business, the focus has been on delineating the difference between the two groups. The successful business people are the ones who have access to all the resources that the world has to offer and they also know how to use these resources. They have the knowledge and the information to use them in the right manner. They know how best to utilize their time. They know how to build networks. Most importantly, they know how to identify their niches and tap into the vast potential that a targeted niche can have for their business.

The unsuccessful business person is a very different species. Even the unsuccessful business people have access to all the resources that the successful business people do. But their biggest shortcoming is that they either do not educate themselves or keep themselves informed about these resources and/or they do not want to spare the time and effort to utilize them.

We speak about hotshot business people keeping marketing secrets from the unsuccessful business people. There is a common notion that successful business people grow successful because they are secretive and hence they whittle down the competition by not letting them know about the most important things.

However, this is not entirely true. Today, we live in the age of the

Internet and here everything is out in the open for everyone to use. It is an open field out there. People can use whatever they want to enhance their prospects. In this book we have seen what many, many of these resources are, and we have seen how we can use them to progress our business.

That is the reason we say that the successful business people are not very different from the unsuccessful business people at all. The main difference is simply of where they use their time, i.e. successful business people use every accessory that the unsuccessful business person can use as well, but it is their ignorance or reticence that keeps them away from doing so.

In the present world, the Internet has made it possible for access to every possible resource needed for successful marketing. You can

build your own niche, you can build a niche within a niche, you can tap into an existing demand, you can build a new demand, you can do everything it takes to make yourself super-popular. And, of course, you can do whatever you need to become a successful business person.

The line of distinction between the successful business person and the unsuccessful business person needs to blur. We need to live in unity and harmony with each other, and have a uniform financial situation. This is all the more important today, especially because all of us have similar resources at our disposal, so why should the disparities arise?

We have taken a look at various aspects of the successful business person versus the unsuccessful business person concept and have eventually come to this conclusion.

The differences between the successful business person and unsuccessful business person, though quite profound and pronounced at times, should not exist. The fact is that the successful business person does not use any other resources that the unsuccessful business person does not have access to. The failing of the unsuccessful business person is only in the proper knowledge and implementation of these concepts and tools. That is more the pity because both of them - the successful business person and the unsuccessful business person are on an equal footing to start with.

So, keep this point in mind and move ahead. You need to use the right techniques for your survival and progress. The best part is that even the implementation of these strategies is not a very big deal as you have seen in this book. If you invest the time and make the concerted effort to get where you want to go, nothing should deter you from your path and eventual success.

PART II

The Secret Strategies of Highly Successful Entrepreneurs

In Part II, I have compiled a whole array of strategies that will help you become a much better entrepreneur.

These are business secrets that very few people, and albeit very few aspiring entrepreneurs, know about. With these tips, you will be equipped with the most powerful tools that will help you pave your way towards success.

Also, all the tips are written in simple English. Anyone will be able to understand these tips. I have avoided using heavy business terminologies to make sure that this book caters to everyone. Everything is also presented in a logical and easy-to-understand manner. I have also arranged the tips so that they are progressive in nature.

The first part of this book dealt with the mindset of an entrepreneur and we looked at some strategies and business development techniques used by the top entrepreneurs. This second part will show you how to think like a businessman and how to plan and prepare for every aspect of your business.

The second part is technical in nature. However, these tips are also written in simple English. The first section will teach you how to make the correct preparations prior to opening a business and the succeeding parts will teach you marketing, advertising, managing, risk-management, and other miscellaneous strategies.

Chapter 11: How to Think Like A Successful Entrepreneur

1. Have a keen eye for opportunities

Successful entrepreneurs have one thing in common – they have a keen eye for opportunity. When an entrepreneur looks at the world, he sees it differently. He sees 'business opportunities'. For example, when a subdivision has no supermarket nearby, a normal person complains. But an entrepreneur sees profit – an opportunity to open a profitable convenient store. Keep your eyes open for such opportunities and have the courage to grab it.

2. Practice careful optimism

Be optimistic. This means that you should have a positive outlook. A positive thinking brings forth many possibilities. However, optimism can lead to problems if misused. Do not let your 'optimism' blind you from seeing problems just because you want to have a positive way of thinking. Be optimistic. However, you should exercise 'carefulness' at the same time. This is careful optimism.

3. Practice positive pessimism

Pessimism is not all that bad. In business, it has its uses. Pessimism allows one to assume potential problems even before they take place. It might sound crazy, but an entrepreneur should practice some degree of pessimism. However, this pessimism should only be used to 'identify problems'. This pessimism is to be practiced with the positive thought that any problem that will arise will be resolved. Entrepreneurs that have a keen eye for risks possess this ability.

4. Think ahead

A normal person sees only the present time. But an entrepreneur thinks ahead and imagines in his mind what the following days have in store. And to do this, an entrepreneur puts into account things like current news, trends, patterns of changes, and such. Because an entrepreneur knows what to anticipate, he also knows how to take advantage of the situations for his own benefit (ex. An entrepreneur bought a piece of land cheaply. He did this after learning that the area will soon be developed. The development will cause the value of the land to increase in the future).

5. Practice prudence

An entrepreneur never takes steps without thinking things over first. This is called prudence. An entrepreneur does not recklessly jump into a business venture. He does not make business decisions based on whim. An entrepreneur researches first, conducts a study, and thinks things over before taking action. All moves he makes have reasons behind them.

Chapter 12: Plan Like A Successful Entrepreneur

1. Do not jump into anything without doing a study

A real entrepreneur does not decide the possible profitability of a business venture by 'hunch' alone. Yes, the best entrepreneurs have the best 'hunches'. But even so, they make sure that their business idea undergoes thorough feasibility study first. A feasibility study serves many purposes. But first and foremost, it tells the entrepreneur if a business idea is likely to 'fail' or succeed'. A feasibility study also allows an entrepreneur to assume possible difficulties and possible solutions to problems. You can hire a professional to conduct a feasibility study for you if you are not familiar with the procedures.

2. Know the demography of your target customers

As an entrepreneur, you will be part of the so-called 'supply' chain. You will be supplying the 'demands' of your customers-to-be. Therefore, it is necessary that you know the demography of your target customers. For example, once you have identified that your target customers are women between the ages 16-30 that lives in the United States, you will then need to ask the following questions: How many are they? How many of them will want to avail your products/services? How many of them can afford your prices? How many of them have the means to pay (PayPal, credit card, etc.)? By obtaining this information, you will have a better idea how many people will likely buy from you.

3. **Establish a contingency account**

Before you start a business, you will need to conclude how much you will need for the start-up costs. Once you have concluded how much money you will need, it is advisable that you add a 'contingency' budget to the total amount. Ideally, the contingency account is 5% to 10% of the established start-up costs. For example, if you have concluded that you will need $10,000 to start your business, make sure that you start your business with at least $11,000 in capital.

4. **Establish budget for initial months' expenses**

In most cases, businesses are not expected to make income during its first few weeks to first few months of operation (could be up to a year or more in some industries). In some cases, the business may even incur losses in the beginning. As such, it is necessary that you allot a budget to cover your expenses during the 'no income' period. Examples of such expenses include utilities, rent expense, mortgage instalments, salary expense, and others.

5. **Know the characteristics of your target customers**

What characteristics should you look for? These include age, gender, financial capability, and in the case of online marketers, internet usage as well. But more than anything else, you should want to know the interests of your target customers. To achieve such information, you may need to do a study. Use the information to attract the attention of your target customers (ex. Your target customers are teenage girls living in Japan.

Your study revealed that teenage girls in Japan are currently into Gothic Lolita fashion. As an online seller of clothes, you decided to include Gothic Lolita dresses in your list of products in order to attract more Japanese teenagers.)

6. Establish a scope of service

You should set current boundaries. For example, are you planning to extend your services to all States? Or, you are planning to sell only in select States? And if you are an online seller of clothes, will you be selling all clothes for everyone? Or, are you planning to sell only women's clothes, men's clothes, children's clothes, formal wear, casual wear, etc.? Of course, you may extend your scope of service in the future.

7. Make a list of external stakeholders

What are stakeholders? These are groups, organizations, firms, and individuals that your business will have a connection to during its course of operation. These include suppliers, service providers, creditors, and others. Before you start a business, you should make a list of your stakeholders first. Contact them and make an agreement with them. If you will be selling computer accessories for example, you should contact several suppliers first. Discuss business matters with them. Can they supply you continuously? Are they willing to give you discounts? Are they prepared to give you exclusivity for a territory? You may also want to make a list of lending firms so you know where to get additional funds when you need it.

8. Establish a well-planned organizational chart

Are you going to hire people to be a part of your business? If so, you will need to make an organizational chart. This will define the flow of command and authority among your employees (who's on top and who's below). It must be clear who makes the decisions, who reports to whom, who follows who, and such. This will avoid confusion.

9. Deliberate on the requirements for each job position

Now that you have an organizational chart, the next step is to set a list of qualifications for each job position. For example, what qualifications do you think your webpage administrator should have? Should he be knowledgeable in WordPress? Should he have experience in sales? Make sure that each job position is handled by a qualified person. This is important if you want your business to succeed.

10.   Decide on modes of receiving payment

How should your customers pay you? When choosing a mode of payment, you have to make sure that enough choice is available and accessible to your target customers. For example, it may not be feasible to offer PayPal only as a mode of payment if half of your target customers have no access to PayPal. In which case, you may need to offer several payment methods.

11. Establish a business growth projection

You may want to start small in the beginning. Also, you may have set some limits in the scope of service. However, you must also make plans for future growth. If you are starting as a seller of adults' clothes for example, you may want to make plans for selling children's clothes too in the future. Try to imagine what your business will be like after a year, after three years, after five years, and after ten years.

12. Know the law

The law has provisions on how entrepreneurs should run their business. Make sure that you are aware of these laws. For example, you may have to register for tax returns and request permits. And because these laws differ from country to country, state to state, region to region, you may need to research your locality's laws. And if you will be selling products to different countries, you have to know that it is illegal to sell some items in some countries. Make sure that you know what these countries and what these products are.

13. Plan an effective entry to the market

When you enter the market, make sure that you are noticed. Unless you are noticed, your business may not get customers. How do you do this? In an online setting, online merchants usually use the following methods: Press Release submissions, Social Media advertisement, sponsored advertisement, Search Engine Optimization (SEO), email marketing, popups, and others.

Chapter 13: Manage Like A Successful Entreprenuer

1. **Delegate tasks effectively**

As the owner, it is not necessary for you to do everything. You can delegate difficult tasks (ex. Managerial tasks) to other people. This will allow you to do more things (ex. Focus on planning for your business' growth). But delegation is a two-edged sword. If done correctly, it can do your business good. If done wrongly, it can be the downfall of your business. Make sure that you delegate tasks to the right people. Also, make sure that tasks are properly sorted among your employees. Make sure everyone knows their boundaries. This will avoid confusion as well.

2. **Learn how to micro-manage your team**

Although you are delegating tasks, your input is still necessary. Do not let your managers and your employees do all the work. Your presence is still important. You have to supervise them every now then. This way, you will always know what is going on in your business. You will be able to see when a problem or a potential problem presents itself. And although you do not want to doubt your employees, micro-management will prevent the possibility of human error, dishonesty, and internal fraud.

3. Motivate your team to perform

You employees are human. They are not perfect. Even the best people feel demotivated at some point. This is especially true with repetitive work. To keep your employees working at their best, it is important that you add some motivation. There are many ways to do this. One popular method is the awarding of incentives to the best performers. Also, providing your employees with the best tools and equipment to work with will help them do a better job (ex. Better computers, clean office, complete supply, etc.). Think of ways on how to motivate your team.

4. Keep records

What are the things you need to keep a record of? As a basic requirement, all businesses should furnish financial statements. You should also keep a record of your supplies, merchandise, assets, purchase activities, and sales activities. You should also record the hours worked (if applicable) of your employees. This data will be useful to you when making an analysis.

5. Analyze reports/data regularly

Reports include financial statements, inventory counts, employee performance, customer feedback, etc. Basically, any data or report that has to do with your business. Read through these reports and analyze them. Use this data as a reference in your decision-making. When ordering your next batch of merchandise for example, you can refer to your sales data to see which items to order less and which items to order more. These reports exist for a reason. Use them.

6. **Establish a thorough auditing routine**

This is especially important if you are dealing with a lot of merchandise. However auditing is basic to all businesses. Auditing includes cross checking receipts with sales records, conducting inventory counts, doing quality check (equipment and operation), and such. You need to do quality checks regularly to see if anything needs replacing or maintaining. You also need to do internal audits to detect errors and prevent internal fraud.

Chapter 14: Advertise and Promote Like A Successful Entrepreneur

1. Know how to capture the attention of your target customers

An advertisement informs. But a good and effective advertisement moves people to buy. How do you make advertisements like that? First, you need to know the interest of your customers. If you know the very thing/s that will catch the attention of your customers, then you have what you need (ex. A seller of a vitamin supplement product knows that many of its target customers are concerned with beauty. As such, the seller focuses on advertising the benefits of its products to beautification).

2. Decide on the most effective advertisement channels

What are advertisement channels? These are your means of delivering your sales pitch to your target customers. In an online business setting, advertisement channels commonly include submission sites (article submission, video submission, audio submission, etc.), social media sites (Facebook, Twitter, YouTube, etc.) emailing, popups, sponsoring, and so forth. How do you decide which channels to use? It all depends on what channels your target customers are mostly exposed to. For example, if you target customers who are internet-savvy people, perhaps they are most likely exposed to Facebook much of the time, using Facebook as one of your advertisement channels would be a good idea. Take note that it is not necessary to utilize all channels. You only need to utilize the ones that are necessary.

3. Use Facebook to reach customers

Facebook really maximized its potential for providing support to online merchants. Facebook offers unique and comprehensive advertisement tools that allow you to target specific niches (age groups, interest groups, gender groups, etc.)

4. Use Twitter to reach customers

Twitter is like a real-time newsfeed site that spurts out new information by the minute. This makes a great way to communicate with your customers and target customers. If your target customers are likely to be Twitter users (people living in the city, people who like technology, etc.), then using Twitter would be a good way to reach your customers.

5. Apply SEO techniques to boost your webpage's visibility

SEO or Search Engine Optimization is a technique used by online merchants to increase traffic (visits and views) into their website. It makes a website 'more visible' by making the website have a better chance of appearing on the top search results of search engines such as Google and Yahoo. There are many SEO techniques and it is advisable to use all of them. But this is complicated stuff so it is better to hire someone to do this for you.

Chapter 15: Do Marketing Like A Successful Entrepreneur

1. Learn the importance of 'packaging'

When choosing between two different brands, what are your criteria for choosing? Usually, you would likely pick the one with the 'better packaging'. How does this apply to online business? In an online setting, the 'packaging' will be the appearance of your website. When selling products online, it applies to the photographs, text descriptions, and overall page presentation of your products. Therefore, it is important that you invest a lot of quality into 1) the appearance of your website, 2) the photos of your product/s, 3) the text description that comes with your product/s and 3) the overall presentation of your products in your website.

2. Promote your website through submission sites

These include article submission sites, video submission sites, and image submission sites among others. By submitting articles, videos, and images that tell about your website, your services, and your products/services, you are effectively promoting your business on the World Wide Web. It makes you 'more visible'. Hire someone to do this for you.

3. **Acquire meaningful customer feedbacks**

If you get good feedbacks from some of your customers, make sure that you post their feedbacks on your website. This is 'evidence' that your products/services are good. But here is the dirty secret that most online entrepreneurs will not tell you: you can fabricate these feedbacks and no one will know.

4. **Make your website 'appealing'**

If your website is 'appealing', people will likely visit again. How do you make your website 'appealing'? Well, there are many ways. The most common is to make sure that the website layout and graphics design is top notch. You can also add some extras which your specific target niche will love (ex. If your target customers are teenage girls, you should probably use a graphics design that will appeal most to this group).

5. **Establish a 'name brand'**

This is the dream of every entrepreneur - they want the name of their business or the name of their product to become iconic. Examples of iconic brands include Google, Windows, Colgate, and such. When you achieve 'brand' status, you will become the first choice of customers despite the presence of competition. How do you do this? By maintaining good service and quality consistently and unfalteringly, people will soon recognize you.

6. **Hire ghost blog writers**

Look for blog sites and forum pages that talk about the industry you are in (ex. If you are selling stuffed toys, you should look for blog sites and forums where enthusiasts of stuffed toys share info with each other). Then hire ghost writers to post positive comments as though they are satisfied customers of yours. This way, other readers of those blog sites and forums might just be convinced to buy from you as well.

7. Offer discounts once in a while

This is a good chance to gain new customers. If you offer a discount, new people will buy from you. This way, you are giving them the chance to see your products and your services. If they like it, they will surely come back. Also, offering discounts will make your current customers happy.

8. Offer promos once in a while

Promos are different to discounts. The most common is the Buy 1 Get 1 Free promo. Just like discounts, promos are also designed to attract new customers and keep your current customers happy. Of course, you have to make sure that your promo offers are known to your target customers. Advertise in advance that you will be offering a promo offer.

9. Obtain email address of current customers

When a customer buys from you, always give them the chance to provide you their email address. This can be included in the purchase process (make sure that you do not make it compulsory because some customers do not want to share this information). This way, you can inform them by email when you have promo offers or discount sales. Take note however that this is also a double-edged sword. Avoid crowding your customer with emails. If you do, they might just begin to dislike you and find you annoying.

10. Offer freebies that cost little or nothing

Customers love freebies. And by offering freebies, you will also attract new customers. But there is one downside to this: it is costly to give things away for free. So what do you do? One clever solution is to offer a freebie that will cost you little or nothing. Examples include reports, books and other electronic goods that can be redistributed endlessly. And if you have old merchandises that are not getting sold, you can dispose of them by offering them as freebies.

11. Maintain quality even in seemingly unrelated things

Everything in your website must have good quality. They do not have to be extravagant. They just have to be error-free. For example, you must avoid mishaps in graphical editing and grammatical errors in product descriptions. This is because customers will relate any error to the quality of your products/services. If a customer sees many grammatical error in your website for example, that customer will think that you do not value quality. They will also think that your products/services also lack quality.

12. Prioritize on customer satisfaction

Customers return because they liked something about your service. And this is not just about the quality of the product they bought from you. This is about the service you provided in general (ex. How easy it was to transact with you, how fast you had the products delivered, how easy it was to use your website, how informative your product descriptions were, etc.).

Chapter 16: Manage Like A Successful Entrepreneur

1. Analyze which products lack in supply

Following a few weeks or months since you started your operation, you will start to get a good idea on which products sell more and which products sell less. Simply analyze the sales report and sales data. If you see that a certain product is lacking in supply (always ends up as 'out of stock' because a lot of people are buying it), you should increase your order of that product. Apart from the obvious - losing profits, customers get dissatisfied when they want to buy something and keep getting told that the product they want is out of stock. It affects customer satisfaction.

2. Analyze which products are excessive in supply

The next time you resupply, you should order less of the items that are 'excessive' in supply (few people are buying them, such that there are always many left over in your inventory). In some cases, you may even have to remove that item from your list of products. Take note that unsold merchandise is bad for business. It will affect your sales because your investment in that unsold merchandise did not result in profit.

3. **Re-analyze demographic of buyers of particular products**

After a month of operating, start analyzing the demographics of the customers buying your products, including age, gender, nationality, sex, locality etc. This will help you make necessary changes. For example, if you originally perceived your products will sell more to people between ages 16-29 and yet your second study revealed that your buying customers are between the ages of 14 to 40, you could consider increasing the scope of your advertisement to reflect this.

4. **Update future orders according to sales analysis**

Your future orders of merchandise from your suppliers should not be based on guesswork. It should be influenced by current data you have with you – the sales report analysis. The idea is simple: order more products that sell a lot and order less of the products that sell less. Also, you should determine from the sales analysis which products are seasonal (sells well only during certain periods of the year). In which case, you should only order seasonal products during their season.

5. **Acquire supplies by consignment as much as possible**

There are two ways of acquiring merchandise: 1) by purchasing and 2) by consignment. With consignment, you are taking possession of the products but you are not yet paying for them. And here is the juicy part – you will only pay for the sold products. As for the unsold products, you can return them to the supplier if you like. This way, you are not absorbing the losses resulting from the unsold merchandise. It is your supplier that will be absorbing the losses.

6. **Limit orders of introductory products**

At some point in time, you may want to introduce new items into your line of products. But do not get too excited so as to order one too many of the new item. Start with less. If the entire consignment gets sold, then order more next time. If the new item keeps showing promise, it is by then that you can start ordering more on a permanent basis. This is a precaution that professional entrepreneurs always take. This is done to prevent possible losses arising from unsold merchandise.

7. **Do upselling effectively**

Upselling is a marketing technique used by entrepreneurs to maximize sales. This is done by offering additional related products to customers that buy from you. For example, if a customer buys a digital camera from you, you can offer him the chance to also buy related add on products such as memory cards, lenses, tripod stands, and such, perhaps at a discounted price. It would be easier for him to agree to such offers at that point because the products are related to the product they just bought.

8. **Do cross selling effectively**

Cross selling is very similar to upselling. It is done by offering customers the choice to buy more than what they are already purchasing. But in cross selling, you are offering a product that is not related to the one they purchased. For instance, if a customer bought a camera, offering him the option to purchase a DVD player (most likely at a discount of some sort) is called cross selling. This is helpful if you are selling a variety of products that are not related to each other.

Chapter 17: Manage Risk Like A Successful Entrepreneur

1. Make a list of possible 'risks'

Business does not always go according to plan. There are definitely going to be some obstacles and difficulties. But with careful planning, deliberation, and observation, you can come up with a list of possible risks. Try to think of possible problems that your business might face. Try to simulate situations in your head. What difficulties do you think will arise? With this kind of anticipation, you will be better equipped to face such problems as and when they occur.

2. Observe risks faced by competitors

Observe other businesses that offer similar products/services. Normally, these would be your competitors. Look at their history. What problems did they face? What risks did they have to deal with? What risks are they currently having difficulty with? And also, how did they solve the problems that they encountered? These will help you get an idea on how to deal with the risks that you will be facing. Let the experience of others guide you.

3. Have a professional analyze 'risks' for you

Risk analysis is a specific subject. There are professionals trained to do this kind of job. Normally, people with a Degree in business or marketing related subjects have some training in this area. Of course, you do not need to hire someone to do this for you. Maybe the manager or one of the employees you hired can do this. If your business has not opened yet, make sure that you include 'knowledge on risks' as one of the requirements when hiring a manager.

4. Make a game plan (solution) in advance

Once you have identified the possible risks, it is now time to formulate theoretical solutions. What will you do if any of those risks actually arise? Well, you should already have a game plan set in advance. You want to be prepared for any possible risks that might come your way.

5. Take steps to prevent anticipated risks

You may already have a game plan on what to do if a risk comes your way. But there is a better solution – prevention. You should take time to think about the actual steps that will prevent those risks from even occurring in the first place. As they say, prevention is better than cure (ex. If you anticipate that any negative comments that may appear on your Facebook account will affect your business, then you should have a plan to have them removed as soon as possible once they are posted).

Chapter 18: Grow Your Business Like A Successful Entrepreneur

1. Absorb a portion of your earnings as additional capital

The net income (earnings minus all the expenses and costs including employee salary, taxes, rent, etc.) arising from your business is definitely the fruits of your labor. This is the part of the income that will become yours – an amount that you can withdraw for personal use. However, there are times when an entrepreneur refuses to make a withdrawal (or refuses to make a full withdrawal). This is because they return the net income to the business as 'additional investment'. This is how businesses grow.

2. Make a proposal to financial firms

Having your business absorb a portion of your net income is one way to grow your business. But there is another method – borrow additional investment from lending firms. This is a good choice to make if you need a larger amount of money. And if your business is a corporation (limited company) in structure (as registered legally), this is a safer choice.

3. **Think of additional products/services you can offer**

Another way to grow your business is to offer more services/products than you already do. If you are selling computers for example, you can expand your business by offering other electronic products as well (ex. Digital cameras, MP3 players, etc.). Ideally, your new products should still be somewhat related in nature to your current products.

If you want to offer a completely new set of products (ex. you sell computers and you want to start selling beauty products), it is advisable that you open a separate online store for the new products.

4. **Increase your scope of suppliers**

As much as you want to be loyal to your supplier/s, it is not how business really works (unless you signed an exclusivity contract with your supplier). You should still keep your eyes open for the possibility of acquiring new suppliers. Always keep searching. Why? Because you might find suppliers that offer lower prices than your current suppliers. Acquiring merchandise at a lower price means higher income for you. Of course, there are other things to consider such as quality. Ask questions like "though this supplier is cheaper, are his products the same if not better in quality?" And also there is the possibility that one supplier could close down, what will you do then.

5. **Increase your scope of target customers**

Simply put, you should offer products/services that also cater to other demographics. If you are currently offering products to women for example, maybe you should also start offering products to men as well. Also, if you are currently selling to the US or UK market only, maybe you can think of ways on how to expand your services globally. This is a good way to expand your business if you started with a rather limited scope of target customers. Of course, expansion is going to cost more money.

Make sure that you calculate the costs before making such a move. Also, expanding your business is like opening a new business. This means that you will need to do another Feasibility Study before going ahead with that plan. With a Feasibility Study, your plans of expansion will surely take a better, more focused path.

6. Increase your scope of advertisement

Advertising is costly. This is why newly opened businesses often limit the scope of their advertisements in order to save on costs (ex. A business chose to advertise via the Internet only and opted not to advertise via television or even radio or newspaper to avoid costs). But once your business has become more financially stable, you might want to start increasing your scope for advertising in order to invite more customers. And if, up to this point you have only used free advertisement methods, maybe now you can start using paid advertisement tools (note: Facebook for example offers free and paid advertisement tools. Of course, the paid service is more effective and covers a wider scope.).

Chapter 19: Deal with Losses Like A Successful Entrepreneur

1. Offer obsolete products as freebies

Despite precautions, you will still experience some failures. For example, you might have ended up ordering a batch of items that did not get sold. So what do you do? You can use these unsold merchandise to fuel your promotional activities. Why not offer those unsold items for free? Customers love freebies and they dig it. You can also offer unsold items as a 'Buy 1 Take 1 Item' ('Buy 1 Get 1 Item Free in the UK) for some of your products (ex. You are a seller of cameras, however, there is a batch of tripods you ordered but they are not selling. Therefore, you decide to offer the tripods as a Buy 1 Take 1 item for your cameras (giving away a free tripod with every camera).

2. Offer obsolete products at a discount

Another way to dispose of obsolete products and any other products that are not selling is to offer them at a discount. If a product is really struggling, you can sell it at a bigger discount (50% off or 70% off). It does not matter if you cannot profit from these struggling products. What is important is to get back the investment, at least a portion of the investment made on those failed products. When you see shops offering big discounts up to 80% off, it is more than likely that it is because they are trying to dispose of obsolete merchandise.

This is a method that has been in use by businesses for a very long time already.

3. Include obsolete products in 'package deals'

Let us take again the example of the camera and the memory cards that won't get sold. One solution is to offer the two products in a bundle. So to say, you are including a free memory card in a package of the camera. Of course, you would have to add up the price (ex. Camera price is $100 and the memory card is $20 so the combined price of the bundle is $120). This way, customers that want to buy your camera will have no choice but to also pay for the memory card. But this is a risky take. You have to make sure that your customers want the main product badly enough so as to be willing to pay for the bundled secondary item as well. However, good entrepreneurs can make the cost of the overall bundle less noticeable.

4. Include contingency for losses when pricing items

An entrepreneur always assumes that a portion of his/her products will not get sold due to a number of factors (ex. Factory defect, damage from nature, unseasonal item, etc.). So when pricing your item, you should include a contingency for losses. So if you originally planned to sell your product at $120 for example, maybe you should sell it at $121 or $122 dollars instead. The additional $1 or $2 dollars is for the possible losses. Of course, this step is not necessary to products that proved to be a 'sold out' all the time. Applying this concept is especially useful when introducing a new product. This is because you still cannot say for sure if the new product will sell or not.

Chapter 20: Minimise Production/Operation Costs Like A Successful Entrepreneur

1. Do what you can on your own

As an entrepreneur, you will definitely hire people to run your business. But if you can conveniently do some of the tasks, maybe you should shoulder those tasks yourself. This will save you salary costs. For example, if you think that paying for a manager is too costly for you at the moment, you can simply take up the responsibility yourself. And some time in the future when your business becomes more profitable, maybe you can hire a manager to take the task off your shoulders at that time. Until then, you should try to do what you can on your own.

2. Outsource tasks instead of hiring new employees

Some tasks are seasonal (done only occasionally at certain times of the year). Examples include website maintenance, graphics design for webpages, article writing, etc. For such tasks, it is best to just outsource the task. This way, you can avoid additional costs that come with hiring new employees (bonuses, 13th month pay, government contributions, VAT, tax, etc.).

Chapter 21: Miscellaneous Tips for An Entrepreneur

1. **Stay updated in your line of business**

Let us say for example that you sell computers online. In which case, you should keep yourself updated about the latest in the world of computers. You should know the latest operating systems. You should know the latest hardware products, the latest software products, and so on. But more than anything else, you should know which products are trending the most – those that people want the most. This way, you will be able to update your line of products and make sure that you always offer the latest in the market. You will not be left out or worse left behind.

2. **Always be aware of changes that will affect your business**

External changes will sometimes have an impact on businesses. This is especially true concerning economic changes. For instance, the recent economic problem faced by the US caused many businesses to suffer. Also, the recent decree in the Philippines that banned the use of plastic bags caused bankruptcy on many businesses that deal with plastic products. Always be aware of such changes. It is better if you learn about them even before they occur. This way, you will be able to take necessary steps to minimize the negative effects on your business. Of course, you also have to keep your eyes open for changes that will open new opportunities for your business.

3. Keep watch of your competitors

Always keep an eye on the activities of your competitors. Check out the promotional activities that they are utilizing. Check out their growth. Also, check out their prices and it should go without saying, check out their products. Then ask yourself questions such as, do I still have the edge over them? What can I do to top their performance? What changes do I need to make to keep my place in the market?

4. Protect your business secrets

Last but not least by any means.

Let us say for example that your prices are lower than the prices of your competitors. This is your competitive edge. You managed to offer lower prices because you found a supplier that offers very low prices. But what do you think will happen if your competitors learn about your supplier? If they manage to get your supplier, they will also be able to lower their prices. It is these kinds of business secrets that you must protect no matter what. Also, make sure that your employees are sworn to the same degree of secrecy. The importance of business secrets is so big, that the practice of industrial espionage is utilized by many organisations, with the attempts made by one competitor to obtain the secrets of another/others.

CONCLUSION

There is no certainty in business. Even the best entrepreneurs fail from time to time. Even prestigious businessmen suffered failures. But with these tips, you will definitely be able to lower the chances of failure.

If you apply all the strategies you have learnt in this book, you will be able to see problems before they happen. This way, you will be able to take necessary steps that will either prevent the problem from occurring altogether or from causing significant damage.

Of course, the strategies will be difficult to remember. It is advisable that you keep a copy of this book as a reference at hand and refer to it again and again whenever the need should arise.

This is the best way to instill the principles of this book to your mind.

And if this is your first time venturing into business, it is advisable that you start small first. Do not jump into making very big investments. This is because you are still learning. And no book in the world can teach you everything, much learning will come from your own experiences.

Take note that experience is still the best teacher. And this is especially true in doing business. So start small first and learn, keeping in mind failure is a crucial part of learning in business. Once you gain more experience, you can then aim for higher goals.

109

Also, use this book as a reference. Do not base your decision solely on it. The world of business is governed by many 'unpredictable things'. Therefore, you have to act based on the situation and the environment around you.

This book is not a solution to the problems that you will face as a businessman. Rather, this book is designed to provide you with the tools to make you a better businessman – the kind of businessman that can prevent or handle problems based on the situation at any given time.

Hopefully, this book has instilled a positive attitude in you and now you know that you can reach beyond just the very low - hanging fruits and move on to bigger things - make the leap into the hallowed community of the successful business people that you have always been so envious about and wondered what magical touch they had and you didn't.

Good luck with your business venture. Never stop dreaming and keep aiming high.

I wish you all the best for all your future endeavors!